**ENGLISH
TOURING
THEATRE**

A Young Vic/ETT co-production

Been So Long

Book & lyrics **Che Walker**
Music & lyrics **Arthur Darvill**

Been So Long

Yvonne **Naana Agyei-Ampadu**
Gil **Harry Hepple**
Raymond **Arinze Kene**
Barney **Omar Lyefook**
Simone **Cat Simmons**

Backing vocals
Gemma Knight Jones
Jenessa Qua
Samantha-Antoinette Smith

Band
Arthur Darvill
Nigel Darvill
Dominic Goundar
Paolo Minervini

Direction **Che Walker**
Composer/Musical direction **Arthur Darvill**
Design **Dick Bird**
Lighting **Jon Clark**
Sound **Paul Arditti**
Choreography **Bonnie Oddie**
Fight direction **Kevin McCurdy**
Casting **Pippa Ailion**
Assistant director **Laura McCluskey**

Stage manager **Julia Reid**
Deputy stage manager (Young Vic) **Jenny Grand**
Deputy stage manager (Edinburgh) **Susie Jenkins**
Assistant stage manager **Rebecca Ridley**
Costume supervisor **Hattie Barsby**
Wardrobe maintenance **Jo Green**
Sound operator (Young Vic) **Daniel Higgott**
Sound operator (Edinburgh) **Dominic Bell**
Technical stage manager (ETT) **Andy Stubbs**

Set built in Young Vic workshop by Paul Halter, Emma Heywood, Will Wyld, John Sweales, Tom Pattullo, Danah Holmes-White, Gibson Arpino.

Special thanks to
Fabian Spencer – Additional rap lyrics 'Man of Steel'
Alex Lanipekun – Additional rap lyrics 'Girls' Night Out'

Che Walker Book, lyrics & direction

Writing credits include: *The Frontline* at Shakespeare's Globe; *Flesh Wound* and *Been So Long* (the play) at the Royal Court (Winner of the George Devine Award); *Crazy Love* for Paines Plough; *Car Thieves* at the National Studio.

Directing credits include: *Rootz Spectacular* at the Belgrade Theatre; *Achidi J's Final Hours, Etta Jenks* (Finborough Theatre); *Macbeth* (Southwark Playhouse); *Balm in Gilead, Mouthful of Birds* (RADA).

Arthur Darvill Music, lyrics & musical direction

Music credits include: *The Frontline* by Che Walker (Shakespeare's Globe); *50 Ways to Leave Your Lover* (Bush); *50 Ways to Leave Your Lover at Christmas* (Bush); *Stoopud Fucken Animals* by Joel Horwood (Traverse Theatre); *Public Display of Affection* by Joel Horwood (Nabokov); *Crazy Love* by Che Walker (Paines Plough); Broken Space Season – Including: *St Petersberg & A Series of Ghost Stories* (Bush Theatre); *Artefacts* by Mike Bartlett (Nabokov/Bush); *Suddenly Last Summer/Timon of Athens/A Doll's House* (RADA). Upcoming projects include *Sudden Loss of Dignity* (Bush) and the Time Cats.

Acting credits include: Film: *Pelican Blood* (Ecosse); *Sex & Drugs & Rock & Roll* (New Boots and Panties 2).

Television credits include: *Little Dorrit* (BBC); *He Kills Coppers* (Ecosse).

Theatre credits include: *Terre Haute* (Nabokov); *Swimming With Sharks* (Vaudeville); *Stacy* (Arcola).

Arthur is an Artistic Associate of the Bush Theatre.

Dick Bird Design

Theatre includes: *La Grande Magie* (Comedie Francaise); *Lear* (Crucible, Sheffield); *Othello, As You Like It* (Shakespeare's Globe); *The Enchanted Pig, How Much is Your Iron?, The Three Musketeers, Monkey!* (Young Vic); *Little Match Girl* (Tiger Lilies Tour); *Tejas Verdes, Marathon* (Gate); *The Night Season, The Walls, A Prayer for Owen Meany* (National); *Harvest, Flesh Wound* (Royal Court); *Rabbit, Heavenly, Dirty Wonderland, Peepshow* (Frantic Assembly); *The Wind in the Willows, The Lady in the Van* (West Yorkshire Playhouse); *Light* (Theatre de Complicite); *Closer, My Fair Lady* (Teatro Nacional, Buenos Aires); *Icarus Falling, Vagabondage* (Primitive Science).

Opera includes: *Snegurochka* (Wexford Festival Opera); *Street Scene* (Young Vic); *Un Segreto D'Importanza* (Teatro Communale di Bologna); *The Gondoliers* (Oper Am Rhein); *The Gambler* (Opera Zuid, Maastricht); *La Boheme, The Magic Flute* (LSVO, Vilnius); *Thwaite* (Almeida Opera); *Messalina* (Battignano Opera Festival); *Vollo di Notte, Il Tabarro* (Long Beach Opera Company).

Jon Clark Light

Theatre includes: *The Winter's Tale, The Merchant of Venice* (RSC); *Women of Troy* (National Theatre); *Street Scene, The Jewish Wife, How Much Is Your Iron?* (Young Vic); *Aunt Dan & Lemon, The Pride, Gone Too Far!* (Royal Court); *The Birthday Party, Spyski!, Water* (Lyric Hammersmith); *Three Days of Rain* (Apollo); *The Lover & The Collection, Dickens Unplugged* (Comedy); *The Soldier's Tale* (Old Vic); *Pinter's People* (Haymarket); *Eric's* (Liverpool Everyman); *On The Rocks* (Hampstead Theatre); *Night Time* (Traverse, Edinburgh); *Gone to Earth* (Shared Experience).

Opera includes; *Into The Little Hill, Down By The Greenwood Side* (The Opera Group, ROH2); *The Love for Three Oranges* (Scottish Opera & RSAMD), *Jenufa* (revival for ENO, Washington Opera); *Tarantula in Petrol Blue* (Aldeburgh); *I Capuleti e I Montecchi, L'Elisir d'Amore, The Barber of Seville, Cosi Fan Tutte* (Grange Park Opera).

Dance includes: *Libera Me, Between The Clock and The Bed* (Bern Ballett); *Tenderhook, Sorry for the Missiles* (Scottish Dance Theatre), *Anton & Erin* (London Coliseum).

Paul Arditti Sound

Recent sound designs include: *When The Rain Stops Falling* (Almeida); *Mary Stuart* (Broadway); *The Cherry Orchard & Winter's Tale* (Brooklyn Academy of Music, Old Vic); *Billy Elliot the Musical* (Broadway, Melbourne, Sydney, London); *Under The Blue Sky* (Duke of Yorks); *The Diver* (Soho); *Les Liaisons Dangereuses* (Broadway); *The Revenger's Tragedy, Never So Good, Happy Now?, Saint Joan, Market Boy* (National); *The Pain and the Itch* (Royal Court); *Vernon God Little, The Member of The Wedding, The Respectable Wedding, Hergé's Adventures of Tintin* (Young Vic).

Recent awards and nominations: *Mary Stuart* (Tony Award nomination 2009); *Saint Joan* (Olivier Award 2008); *Billy Elliot the Musical* (Tony

Award nomination 2009, Drama Desk Award nomination 2009, Helpmann Award nomination 2008, Olivier Award 2006); *Festen* (Evening Standard Award 2005, Olivier Award nomination 2005); *The Pillowman* (Drama Desk Award 2005, Olivier Award nomination 2004).

Bonnie Oddie Choreography

Bonnie trained at Lewisham College and London Studio Centre where she graduated in 1993.

Committed to providing access to excellence, Bonnie was Founding Artistic Director for East London Dance Youth Co and is currently Artistic Director for Studio Youth, a training ground and performance company for young people in London.

Bonnie has worked extensively as a freelance dancer, teacher and choreographer. Choreographic credits include Intoto Contemporary Dance co, JazzXchange Music and dance Co, *Life on Mars* (Channel 4), site-specific works for The National Gallery and The Royal Festival Hall and her most recent independent work, a comedic piece of dance theatre entitled Boxed-im-Perfect.

Kevin McCurdy Fight direction

Kev is the only Equity professional Fight Director in Wales.

Theatre credits include: *Macbeth; A Midsummer Night's Dream; Romeo and Juliet; The Three Musketeers; Of Mice and Men; Twelfth Night; A View from the Bridge; The Pirates of Penzance; Taboo* (UK tour); *House and Garden; Orange; The Grapes of Wrath; Quadrophenia* (World Premiere); *The Birthday Party; It's Not the End of the World; My Favourite Year; We The People; Killer Joe; West Side Story; Suspension; The Frontline* (World Premiere); *As You Like It.*

Film and television fight direction credits include: For HTV, *Jacob's Ladder, The Chosen;* For BBC: *Belonging, The Story of Tracy Beaker, Hearts of Gold, Carrie's War, Doctor Who Christmas Special, Torchwood;* For S4C: *Pobol Y Cwm, Y Pris, Caerdydd;* For Channel 4: *CCTV;* **Films for TV:** *Arthurs' Dyke; A Way of Life; Arwyr;* **Feature films:** *Life Translated; Intergalactic Combat; The Baker; Season of the Witch.*

Ballet and dance includes: *The Canterville Ghost* (English National Ballet); *Aladdin* (New National Theatre Tokyo); *The Banquet* (Protein Dance).

Pippa Ailion Casting

Pippa has cast over 100 productions for West End, UK, US and internationally. Seasons at Chichester, Crucible Theatre Sheffield & West Yorkshire Playhouse.

She was Resident Associate Director and cast three seasons of fifteen European Classics for Jonathan Miller at The Old Vic between 1987 and 1991.

West End / London includes: *Spring Awakening, Wicked, Marguerite, Chess In Concert, The Drowsy Chaperone, Porgy & Bess, Generations, The Postman Always Rings Twice, Blue Man Group* & Europe, *Follow*

My Leader, The Enchanted Pig, Acorn Antiques & UK tour, *Billy Elliot, Tonight's The Night* & UK tour, *Simply Heavenly, We Will Rock You* & UK tour/Europe, *Disney's Beauty and the Beast* & UK tour, *Japes, Wit, The Lion King* & Europe, *Rent, The Magistrate, Hair, Into the Woods.*
Current UK tours: *Quadrophenia, We Will Rock You, High School Musical* (Paris).
Future: *The Fairy Queen* (Glyndebourne), *The Importance of Being Earnest* (Regent's Park), *Legally Blonde* (West End).

Laura McCluskey Assistant director
Theatre includes: *Gone too Far!* at the Royal Court (Assistant director); *Nina and Shaz* at the Brockley Jack (Playwright/Director).

Naana Agyei-Ampadu Yvonne
Theatre includes: *Caroline or Change* (National); *Avenue Q* (The Noel Coward); *The Frontline* (Shakespeare's Globe); *The Little Shop of Horrors* (The New Wolsey); *Aladdin* (The Hawth Theatre).

Harry Hepple Gil
Theatre includes: *Burnt by the Sun* (National); *I Caught Crabs in Walberswick* (Bush/Pleasance/UK Tour); *Exposure* (3 Mills Studio); *Donnington Castle* (Nabokov); *Toast, Alaska* (Royal Court).

Arinze Kene Raymond
Identity Drama School Best Actor 2006 & 2007.
Theatre includes: *The Lion King* (Disney); *Daddy Cool* (World Tour); *Torn* (Arcola Theatre). **Film includes:** *Freestyle* (UK Film Council).

Gemma Knight-Jones Backing singer
Theatre includes: *Rent* (Broadway Theatre); *Ragtime* (Forest Music Productions); *Hitting Home* (Futures Theatre Company).

Omar Lyefook Barney
Soul legend Omar is the founder of nu-classic British Soul. A graduate of the Guildhall School of Music, he has six albums to his name. With a career spanning over two decades, Omar has won much critical acclaim and has collaborated with numerous high profile artists including Stevie Wonder, Erykah Badu, Common, Angie Stone and Estelle to name but a few.
Omar trained at Identity Drama School, the UK's First Black Drama School.

Jenessa Qua Backing singer
Theatre includes: *Gone with the Wind* (New London Theatre); *Sweet Soul Music* (UK tour); *Show Boat* (Royal Albert Hall); *Blues Brothers* (European tour); *Jack and the Beanstalk* (Cambridge Arts Theatre); *The Road* (Her Majesty's Theatre); *Jerry Springer – The Opera* (NT & West End).

Television includes: *Gone with the Wind* documentary (TCM); *My Body Hell* (Channel 5); *LK Today* (GMTV); *Freddy Mercury Tribute Concert* (BBC), *Royal Variety Performance* (with London Community Gospel Choir).

Cat Simmons Simone

Television includes: *The Bill* (ITV/Talkback Thames); *Family Affairs* (Channel 5); *Holby City, Girls Weekend* (BBC).
Film includes: *Life N Lyrics* (Universal).
Theatre includes: *Aladdin* (The Old Vic); *We Happy Few* (Gielgud Theatre); *Simply Heavenly* (Young Vic); *Jesus Christ Superstar, Whistle Down the Wind* (Really Useful Group).

Samantha-Antoinette Smith Backing singer

Theatre includes: *The Lion King* (Disney); *Mama I Want to Sing* (West End); *Dancin & Singin the Blues* (European tour).
Music tours include: *Mika, Blur, Richard Ashcroft* (European tour); *Erasure, Depeche Mode, Jamiroquai* (World tour).
Recordings include: *Lionel Ritchie, Dave Stewart, Atomic Kitten, The London Community Gospel Choir; Luther Vandross, Beverley Knight.*

Nigel Darvill Keys

As a touring session musician credits includes: *The Fine Young Cannibals, Ruby Turner, Hipsway, Ranking Roger, Edwin Starr, Duane Eddy, Johnny Tillotson.*
Recording credits include: *Ruby Turner, Ranking Roger, Clifford T Ward.*
Writing credits include: *Cadbury's Maynards Sours* commercial.
Composition for Theatre includes: *Cannon Hill Puppet Theatre*, Birmingham.
Music for Film with Midlands Screen commission includes: *Rhubarb & Roses* (Director Ged McGuire); *Hilton Park* (Director Simon Broadley).
Work with advertising agencies and production companies has included music composition for *VW/Audi, British Airways* and *Rolls Royce*.

Dominic Goundar Drums

Theatre includes: *Blood Brothers, Joseph and his Amazing Technicolor Dreamcoat, Tell me on a Sunday* (Kenwright Productions).
Live events include: *Bjorn Again* (Worldwide events); *Sir Cliff Richard* (Hever Castle); *Dancing in the Streets Revue* (Flying Music); *Vince Hill* (Stag Theatre); *James Fox* (Stoke on Trent).
Film includes: *Thomas and the Magic Railroad* – OST (Gullane Entertainment); *Bluebird Entertainment* (Bluebird Productions).
Radio includes: *A Flame in your Heart* (BBC Radio 4).

Paolo Minervini Bass

Television includes: *Roxy Bar* (MTV); *Festival Bar* (Italia Uno); *Ottavo Nano, Piazza Grande* (RAI 2).

THE YOUNG VIC

GREAT SHOWS FOR GREAT AUDIENCES —NOW AND IN THE FUTURE—

Our shows
We present the widest variety of classics, new plays, forgotten works and music theatre. We tour and co-produce extensively within the UK and internationally.

Our artists
Our shows are created by some of the world's great theatre people alongside the most adventurous of the younger generation. This fusion makes the Young Vic one of the most exciting theatres in the world.

Our audience
...is famously the youngest and most diverse in London. We encourage those who don't think theatre is 'for them' to make it part of their lives. We give 10% of our tickets to schools and neighbours irrespective of box office demand, and keep prices low.

Our partners near at hand
Each year we engage with 10,000 local people – individuals and groups of all kinds including schools and colleges – by exploring theatre on and off stage. From time to time we invite our neighbours to appear on our stage alongside professionals.

Our partners further away
By co-producing with leading theatre, opera, and dance companies from around the world we challenge ourselves and create shows neither partner could achieve alone.

The Young Vic is a company limited by guarantee, registered in England No. 1188209.
VAT registration No. 236 673 348
The Young Vic (registered charity number 268876) receives public funding from

'Thank God for the Young Vic.'
The Observer

'You really sense a special mood of open-mindedness at the Young Vic.'
Evening Standard

SUPPORTING THE YOUNG VIC

The Young Vic relies on the generous support of many trusts, companies and individuals to continue our work on and off stage year on year.

For their recent support we thank...

PUBLIC FUNDERS
Arts Council England
Equalities and Human
Rights Commission
Lambeth Arts
Southwark Council

CORPORATE SUPPORTERS
American Airlines
Bloomberg
Cadbury Schweppes
Foundation
De La Rue Charitable Trust
HSBC Bank plc
J.P. Morgan
KPMG Foundation
London Eye
North Square Capital

THE DIRECTORS CIRCLE

BIG CHEESES
HgCapital
Ingenious Media Plc
Land Securities

HOT SHOTS
Bloomberg
Blue Rubicon
Clifforf Chance LLP
Slaughter and May
Symbian
Taylor Wessing LLP

HIGH FLIERS
London Communications
Agency

TRUST SUPPORTERS
Arimathea Charitable Trust
City Parochial Foundation
John S Cohen Foundation
Columbia Foundation Fund
of the Capital Community
Foundation
D'Oyly Carte Charitable Trust
Dorset Foundation
Equitable Charitable Trust
Eranda Foundation
Ernest Cook Trust
Esmée Fairbairn Foundation
Garrick Charitable Trust
Genesis Foundation
Goethe-Institut
Help a London Child
Henry Smith Charity
Jerwood Charitable Foundation
John Ellerman Foundation
The Limbourne Trust
Martin Bowley Charitable Trust
Paul Hamlyn Foundation
Peter Moores Foundation
Pidem Fund
Quercus Charitable Trust
Steel Charitable Trust
The Worshipful Company
of Grocers

FRIENDS OF THE YOUNG VIC

PRODUCTION SUPPORTERS
Michael Barton
Tony & Gisela Bloom
Sandy Chalmers
Kay Ellen Consolver & John
Storkerson
David Day
Eileen Glynn
Chris & Jane Lucas
Nadine Majaro & Roger Pilgrim
Miles Morland
Anda & Bill Winters

BEST FRIENDS
Jane Attias
Chris & Frances Bates
Alex & Angela Bernstein
The Bickertons
Katie Bradford
Conway van Gelder Grant
Sarah Hall
Richard Hardman & Family
Nik Holttum &
Helen Brannigan
Suzanne & Michael Johnson
Tom Keatinge
John Kinder & Gerry Downey
Tim & Theresa Lloyd
Simon & Midge Palley
Charles & Donna Scott
Justin Shinebourne
Richard & Julie Slater
Jack & Joanne Tracy
Leo & Susan van der Linden
Rob Wallace
Edgar & Judith Wallner

GREAT FRIENDS
Angus Aynsley & Miel de
Botton Aynsley
Tim & Caroline Clark
Robyn Durie
Maureen Elton
Jenny Hall
Sheila & John Harvey
Susan Hyland
Tony Mackintosh
Ian McKellen
Frank & Helen Neale
Anthony & Sally Salz
Mr & Mrs Bruce R Snider
Donna & Richard Vinter

HgCapital is proud to sponsor the Young Vic.

HgCapital }

BEEN SO LONG

Book & Lyrics Che Walker

Lyrics and Music Arthur Darvill

OBERON BOOKS
LONDON

WWW.OBERONBOOKS.COM

First published in 2009 by Oberon Books Ltd
521 Caledonian Road, London N7 9RH
Tel: 020 7607 3637 / Fax: 020 7607 3629
e-mail: info@oberonbooks.com
www.oberonbooks.com

A catalogue record for this book is available from the British
Library.

ISBN: 978-1-84002-937-6

Cover photograph by Amy Ashton

Characters

BARNEY
SIMONE
YVONNE
GIL
RAYMOND

Special thanks to

Kay Ellen Consolver and John Storkerson, Matthew Dunster, David Lan and all at The Young Vic, Kerry Michaels, Karen Fisher, Philip Hedley and all at Theatre Royal Stratford East. And a massive thanks to Fabian Spencer for additional rap on 'Man Of Steel' and Alex Lanipekun for additional rap on *Girls' Night Out*, Vivian Acheampong, Yetunde Oduwale, Claire Prempeh, Wunmi Mosaku, Paul Richard Biggin, David Ononokpono, Brad Henshaw, Ngo Omene-Ngofa, Sophia Nomvete, Golda Roshuevel, Johnny Amobi, Kennie Andrews, Chu Omambala, Phoebe Waller-bridge, Gloria Onitiri, Ray Shell, Matt Hill, Ralph Moxon, Naana Agyei-ampadu, Harry Hepple, Arinze Kene, George Eggay, Rachael Macfarlane, Enyonam Gbesemete, Me'sha Bryan, Matthew Newtion, Katie Cooper, Marsha Henry, Paolo Minervini, Dominic Goundar, Nigel Darvill, Ellie Darvill.

Act One

THE BAR PHOENIX

BARNEY polishes glasses.

Song – Love Don't Drink Here

BARNEY   I've been waiting round here for years
I haven't even come up for air
I just wanna call time
On this desperation
Stop measuring my life in optics and drams
Gotta let in the light
Stop being half a man
Cause nothing ever comes my way
No
She don't really care
She don't really care
No, no, no, no,
No, no, no, no,
No, no, no, no, no, no, no.
Love don't drink here any more.
No, no, no, no,
No, no, no, no,
No, no, no, no, no, no, no.
Love don't drink here any more.
I remember when love used to soar
But Love don't drink here any more

Enter GIL, barely twenty.

Evening.

GIL stares at him.

17

What would you like to drink?

GIL Don't like the way you asked me that question.

BARNEY I see.

GIL Summink boutchour tone.

BARNEY My tone?

GIL (*To himself.*) It's time... Yes, yes, it's time...

BARNEY I beg your pardon?

GIL I sense the man...he's close, yes, he's close...

BARNEY Eh?

GIL (*To himself.*) Taste it, Gil, taste it, mate.

BARNEY You getting ready to order a drink?

GIL SHUTCHOUR MOUTH!

BARNEY backs off slightly.

Where is he?

BARNEY Where is who?

GIL Raymond LeGendre.

BARNEY Who?

GIL Raymond LeGendre.

BARNEY Raymond LeGendre...don't know nobody called Raymond LeGendre...

GIL I'M NOT HERE TO BE FUCKED ABOUT! IT IS TIME! I WILL BE DENIED NO LONGER! I HAVE SPENT THREE YEARS TURNING MYSELF INTO THE SHARK THAT BREATHES! (*Suddenly quiet.*) Again I ask you: Where is Raymond LeGendre?

BARNEY I, I, honestly don't know the geeza.

GIL   You're a big fat fuckin liar.

BARNEY   Perhaps if you described the fella. Whass he
             look like?

GIL   Raymond LeGendre? He looks good, man. Tall
             man. Powerful physique. Moves easy, athletic.
             Birds go potty for him. He's relaxed, y'see? He
             makes 'em giggle and drop their drawbridge.
             Splashdown, perennial. He must die.

BARNEY   Wait a minute…I think I know… Geezer used to
             box a little in that gym across the park?

GIL   Thass the one. Geezer keeps hisself well trim.

BARNEY   He used to come in back when we had a crowd.
             Zoomed right on the women. Thass how you'd
             know it was last orders, he'd be pouring a girl
             into her coat and scooping her towards the door.
             Every single night. Different girl, same result.
             Geezer should be in movies or summink.

             Pause.

GIL   Some geezers go through life…I dunno, they
             juss, they juss…flow, y'know? And some geezers
             go through life… They bounce into one brick
             wall after another til they're blind with brain
             damage… Lissen my friend, I'm sorry I put my
             hands on you. Y'wanna bar me, then bar me.
             I'm a wrong 'un. I'm a wrong 'un.

BARNEY   Forget about it.

GIL   Been tryna forget about it for three years. Have
             a drink wimme.

             GIL puts down some money for two drinks.

             BARNEY pours them.

             Cheers.

BARNEY   Cheers.

GIL   Gil.

BARNEY   Barney.

GIL   Easy.

BARNEY   Niceness.

They drain their drinks.

GIL   Ainchou curious as to exackly why I wanna kill Raymond LeGendre?

BARNEY   Not remotely.

GIL breaks down crying.

GIL   He took my girl.
He took my girl
He took my girl
He took my fuckin girl from me.
Any girl he wanted and he took my girl from me.
I only had the one girl…

Song – Been Too Long

I only had the one girl
Creature made my toes uncurl
Lost my love
Lost my angel sent from above
Now my heart is in danger
Cause it's been too long
Since I last saw her face
It's been too long
Since I said goodbye
When I think of her
And I think of her
All the time

I just hang my head and start to
cry (*Repeat.*)

Bad ideas in my head
Got murder on my mind
Gonna take this vengeance out on him
It's him I have to find
He took my girl
He took my girl
He took my girl from me.

(*Rap.*) Gonna hurt the man who stole her
The man who now holds her,
Like I told you, plain soldier
Gonna slice the man
Gonna dice the man
I won't rest til I ice the man
Been stewing in hatred
And simmering in silence
Violence inspires my blood like a virus
I digress

(*Song.*) Cause it's been too long
Since I last saw her face
It's been too long
Since we said goodbye
When I think of her
And I think of her
All the time
I just hang my head and start to cry

BARNEY hands GIL a tissue.

BARNEY   When was all this, Gil, mate?

GIL   July twenny ninth, 2006.

BARNEY   Thass over three years ago.

21

GIL I'm aware of how long iss been…

BARNEY Raymond LeGendre knew it was your missus when he worked it?

GIL Dunno. Don't make no difference. He must die.

BARNEY Look, uh…iss not my intention to denigrate your missus… But consider this…consider this…she betrayed you, knowingly. Of her own volition, mate. Surely she shares the culpability.

GIL Nah, mate. She knew not what she done. Poor girl never stood a chance. The man is a vortex. LeGendre's the one who has to die. Raymond LeGendre.

BARNEY Killing him, though… Bit overstated, innit?

GIL I DIDN'T ASK FOR YOUR COMMENTS!
I didn't ask you to say a word. It's over. My mind is set. It's over. Now. You are gonna pour me another drink and you are not gonna speak no more. And we're gonna sit and wait. For Raymond LeGendre.
Because it is time.
We're gonna wait.
And sit.
In silence.
Silent sitting.

A long pause.

Why is that bar, that Jake's bar, why is Jake's bar, why is that so packed and you ain't got nobody over here? Across the street. Iss packed. Ramup. And the sign outside says you're closing down. Why?

BARNEY does not answer.

You married? Got any kids? Divorced ? You seem kinda heartbroken. You seem kinda closed up. Kinda like you been let down. Kinda like you trapped in a box. Or summink

Pause.

Such a beautiful girl, my girl.

BARNEY does not speak.

Come on, iss ok, talk wimme. Such a beautiful girl, my girl.

BARNEY   There's lotsa girls.

GIL   Not for me. I don't want any other girl, ever. I ain't had a girl since that fateful day.

BARNEY   You ain't had a girl since –

GIL   July twenny ninth 2006.

BARNEY   You not got with a bird since?

GIL   Nope.

BARNEY   Why not?

GIL   I love her, thass why not.

BARNEY   Three years…

GIL   What about you, you in love ?

BARNEY does not answer.

I miss my girl like crazy.

BARNEY   Not surprised, you ain't had your horn tugged in three years…

GIL deflates a little.

Whass her name, this girl?

GIL   Why?

23

BARNEY   Wondering if I might know her.

GIL   You don't know her.

BARNEY   Whass her name?

GIL   Ask Raymond LeGendre what her name is.

BARNEY   I can't if you kill him.

Enter SIMONE and YVONNE. Stylish, beautiful and tough.

Song – Girls' Night Out

SIMONE   Gonna have fun and scandal on a girls'
              night out

YVONNE   Too hot to handle on a girls' night out.

SIMONE AND VYONNE TOGETHER

              Thrills and chills
              Laughs and spills
              Girl, you gimme joke
              White wine and cigarette smoke
              Nobody does it the way we're gonna do it
              We're going out
              We're gonna do it right
              Forget our worries
              And all our duties
              We're gonna get all silly, see
              And shake our booties

YVONNE   (*Rap.*) Got my best garms on I look fly

SIMONE   (*Rap.*) Yvonne, you got changed, like, five
              times

YVONNE   Why tey dat girl, please don't play
              You know I look fresh and trim girl don't
              hate

24

SIMONE	Baby you're crazy
YVONNE	No, I'm mad horny
SIMONE	All dem pretty hood boys juss bore me
YVONNE	My hair done right – toes look cute Believe I'm nang from my head to my boots Dance floor vet !
SIMONE	Dance floor sket
YVONNE	Simone you tweakin – your mouth don't rest
SIMONE	Dat a belt you wearing or a dress ?
YVONNE	I dress to impress Cause I ain't on no night bus flex Drink champagne and smoke dat ses
SIMONE	More like cheap wine and cigarettes I hope we don't see your waste man ex
YVONNE	I hate we don't see my waste man ex !

SIMONE AND YVONNE

> Come on now
> Come on now
> Come on now
> Come on now, what you gon do (*x2*)
> Fun and scandaaaaal

YVONNE	Where's all the menfolk? Dead in here.
SIMONE	Yvonne! You promised.
YVONNE	What?
SIMONE	This night 'bout you and me catchin joke, ain't about the thrill of the chase. I ain't come out

for that. I ain't come out the flat for time and I wanna see you. Iss good to see you.

YVONNE   Me too. Glad you come out your hermitage for the evening, sitchourself down and I'll get 'em in.

YVONNE goes over to the bar.

Y'alright, B?

BARNEY   How you doing, Yvonne?

YVONNE   I'm good, how you doing?

BARNEY   What can I getcha?

YVONNE   Usual, please

YVONNE looks at GIL and smiles at him neutrally.

GIL   (*To YVONNE.*) WHAT THE FUCK ARE YOU LOOKING AT! DON'T FUCKIN LOOK AT ME, RIGHT! I FUCKING HATE BEING LOOKED AT!

YVONNE   I'm juss looking.

GIL   I don't wanna be fuckin looked at.

YVONNE   I'm. Just. Looking.

GIL   Tryna have a, a, a, a, a, a, fuckin conversation here!

YVONNE   I toldjuh already, holdjour space, rest y'self, y' little child.

GIL   BOLLOX! FUCK! I'LL KILL YA!

GIL stands up to strike YVONNE.

YVONNE   So what, so what, so what? Huh? SO what? So whatchou fuckin saying?

SIMONE is behind GIL.

26

SIMONE	You're one a the Scantleburys. Live down on them flats, innit. Got a brother called Luke. Your brother's inside at this moment in time.
YVONNE	Who is this fool, babes?
SIMONE	His brother's the fool. Few years back, he gets hisself a sawnoff and bowls into the halifax on the high street –
YVONNE	He never!
SIMONE	He did, y'know!
YVONNE	His own high street, practically!
SIMONE	He robs the place for a minor total, bowls out big and broad into a sunny afternoon, decides he's hungry, crosses the road and decides to stop in micky d's for a cheeseburger.
YVONNE	Yuh lie.
SIMONE	God is my witness.
YVONNE	This is the Mcdonald's that backs onto the police station?
SIMONE	It gets worse. Rozzers are so stupid, my man woulda made it, but he finishes his burger, belches, wipes his lips and tries to stick the NatWest.

YVONNE cracks up laughing.

No word of it a lie.

YVONNE	(*To GIL.*) Is this true, bubba?
GIL	That is it. My wrath is enraged. I'm gonna batter the both a youse.
SIMONE	You familiar with the crescent, sweety?

27

GIL   Course I'm familiar with the crescent. Used to run that manor.

SIMONE How sweet. Lemme whisper a name in your ear…

SIMONE whispers a name in GIL's ear.

GIL pales.

GIL   Oh.

Pause.

Mate a yours, is he?

SIMONE My cousin.

GIL   Oh.

SIMONE If you leave now, you might salvage a tiny bit a pride. Try coming back when you got some hair on your balls.

GIL makes a painful exit to the door. When he gets to the door, he stops.

GIL   (*To YVONNE.*) You're fuckin lucky.

GIL leaves.

YVONNE Oi, you.

SIMONE What?

YVONNE Don't do that again. Bringing your cousin's name in to it. I don't need to be rescued.

SIMONE I wasn't rescuin you, I was rescuin him. I see that look in your eye before.

YVONNE Telling you… I was about to bruck up that boy for life…

BARNEY comes over with a bottle of champagne.

BARNEY Compliments of the house.

SIMONE   Barney, you're so sweet.

YVONNE   Sweet on you is what he is.

BARNEY   I'm sweet on the both a youse.

YVONNE   Stop frontin, Barney, you're all moon-faced when Simone walks in

BARNEY   Excuse me, but my face is nothing like the moon at any time.

SIMONE   Thanks for the bottle.

BARNEY   Least I could do for you

YVONNE   Is it true you're closing down?

BARNEY   Next Saturday.

SIMONE   End of an era, boy.

BARNEY   Jake's across the road has killed us.

YVONNE   Fucking Jake's, passed it on the way up here, ramup, all the pretty people from MTV.

SIMONE   I hate Jake's.

YVONNE   Me too.

SIMONE   Have a drink with us, B.

BARNEY   I'd like to. Got a few things to do.

SIMONE   Alright then, spit upon our blandishments.

BARNEY   You know it ain't like that.

SIMONE   Take a glass with you, B.

BARNEY   Alright then. L'chaim.

YVONNE   Mud in your eye.

BARNEY retreats to the bar.

Less drink up and head off to Jake's.

SIMONE	You said you hated Jake's.
YVONNE	I do hate Jake's, but I'm horny.
SIMONE	Oh for goodness' sakes… Thought we agreed, tonight ain't about getting hassled by slimy sweaty blokes, tonight meanta be 'bout you and me catching two joke together –
YVONNE	It'll be good for you, a li'l adventure, and you need to know you're a luscious lovely looking female, babe –
SIMONE	Yvonne !
YVONNE	Iss driving me nuts!
SIMONE	But, Yvonne, all the years I know you, you ain't never been good in a relationship
YVONNE	Who said anything about relationships? I ain't lookin relationships, I'm looking hood.
SIMONE	You have not changed…
YVONNE	Wanna take a big bite into a shoulder!
SIMONE	Like a bird of prey.
YVONNE	I want a fella
SIMONE	I grasped that part.
YVONNE	I wish someone would grasp my part. A woman has needs, y'know. I gotta be fulfilled.
SIMONE	Or even filled fully.
YVONNE	I need a man, I'm climbing the walls, I need a man.

Song – I Want a Fella

I want a fella
I want a fella

Make a girl scream and yell-a
I want a fella I want a fella
Make a girl sweet and mellow
Wanna find a man
Wanna grind a man
Gonna hound a man
Gonna pound a man
Inside me, all around me let my body be
your home
Rock me Roll me like my back ain't got no
bone
Tall man short man fat man thin man
Any kinda man juss lemme get a man
To get my teeth in
Lie down beneath him
Unsheathe him
Only thing I won't do is believe him
Get what I want then gettin up and
leave him
A girl has needs
Oh yes indeed
I'm one girl that has a hungry mouth to
feed

(*Spoken over the music.*) Been getting these crazy
fantasies when I been sittin at that fuckin
Apple Mac. My favourite one, right, is that
I'm at the top of Kite Hill, where the wind is
powerful, there's a mighty storm brewing and
swelling, and I'm fuckin this guy, he's a, he's
a wood-spirit, he's a satyr, like Pan, he's got
furry cleft hooves, antlers on his forehead, and
a great tree branch for a dick, y'get me? Even
though he's so strong, I overpower him, throw
him roughly to the cool wet wet grass, I pin
him down, sink my nails into his chest, I squat
bestride his hirsute hips, and I'm juss working

31

him down slowly slowly slowly... I work him
like a winner, and he's roaring and growling
beneath me, I fuck this thing so hard he takes
root into the earth, the storm is juss bucketing
out rain in sheets of sound like John Coltrane,
it's splashing down on my neck, my collarbone,
the soles of my feet, the lightning is flashing
and firing and rending ancient oaks asunder,
the trees groan deeply and crash all around us,
the sky explodes in these exhilarating heavy
booms, and I'm not me no more, I'm a muscle,
rutting and grunting and fucking, I throw back
my head to drink in the storms' rain, and this
bolt of lightning enters me in my mouth, shoots
through the inside of me, and passes through my
body into him through his cock. He arches his
back, tries to escape, but his forearms and feet
have become knotted roots in the earth, and he
dies in an instant, bleeding from his ears, so this
is me, the rain still singing to my nipples, I snap
off his antlers with one twist of my wrist, I jump
on my fuckin mountain bike, naked as the day
I was fuckin born, screaming down Kite Hill,
storm-lashed, holding his bleeding antlers aloft.

Pause.

SIMONE   Sounds lovely.

YVONNE   I want a fella
                  I want a fella
                  I want a fella
                  I want a fella!

Bassline out.

I want a fella

SIMONE   I knew the night would take this turn.

YVONNE	Alright, alright, the fury is passing, ain't no menfolk in this gaff anyways, less juss enjoy our night together.
SIMONE	Enjoy each other's company.
YVONNE	In the here and in the now.
SIMONE	In the here and in the now.

The girls clink glasses.

Enter RAYMOND LEGENDRE.

The band strikes his theme.

Dark suit, no tie.

Tall and handsome, just like GIL said.

Mischief in his swagger.

He gets himself a drink at the bar.

YVONNE	Oh my goodness…
SIMONE	Couldn't do it, couldya? Knew you couldn't do it.
YVONNE	This is mitigating circumstances.
SIMONE	I knew it.
YVONNE	Fashioned from gold and chiseled by thunder.
SIMONE	Craven wench.
YVONNE	What class.
SIMONE	What's the big wow? Just another good-looking man.
YVONNE	Thass a build right there.
SIMONE	Probly works out a little.
YVONNE	Built to work hard.

SIMONE   Brazen.

YVONNE   Pair of buttocks you could balance a plate on.

SIMONE   All your drooling is creating a puddle on the floor.

YVONNE   Thass not my drooling.

SIMONE   Don't do this, baby.

YVONNE   Oh, a decree from the nunnery.

SIMONE   Ain't gonna be the same in the morning, hung over, crusted up, shit for breath, scribbling phone numbers down with two digits judiciously reversed.

YVONNE   I'm goin in, binky.

SIMONE   Ah well. Deal with him.

YVONNE   You gonna be alright, Simone?

SIMONE   I'm always alright. Go get him.

YVONNE walks over to RAYMOND.

YVONNE   Hello, how are you, you look well, I'm feeling fine, good so lissen to this now, I reckon juss once I'd supercede my introverted instincts and grab the bull by the horns... Iss jusst that I look at you, and I do not wanna spend the rest of my life saying What If, y' get me?

Song – Dream

You've got what I need, honey
And I ain't leaving til you're mine, no
I can't wait to see what I dream tonight
I gotta lissen to my instincts
And follow them throooough

34

> I will give you everything if you treat me
> right
> You and I are gonna drink the bar dry
> And disappear into the night
> You and I are gonna set the sky alight
> You and I are gonna drink the bar dry
> And disappear into the night
> Paint the town red
> And set the sky alight

(*Spoken over bassline.*) So what is it you do? Oh no, don't tell me, let me guess, I'm good at this, you're an...actor, Right? You're gonna do well, believe, you got summink makes us women wanna look, and there's a melancholy sweetness keep us looking, makes us wanna nourish you...(*Bassline out.*)

I feel we've made a connection y'know? I feel we're rolling... So, uh, where juh wanna go with this? Where juh wanna take it.

RAYMOND   Who's your friend?

YVONNE   Whatchou say?

RAYMOND   Who's your friend?

Pause.

YVONNE   You have no class, you know that? No fuckin class.

YVONNE storms off and grabs her coat.

As she leaves, she says to SIMONE...

Don't follow me.

YVONNE exits.

RAYMOND walks over to SIMONE.

RAYMOND   I think you're very beautiful.

SIMONE   Whatchou say?

RAYMOND   I think you're very beautiful.

SIMONE   Foolish boyyy…

RAYMOND   Sweet like morning dew.

SIMONE   You muss have a high opinion of y'self to come chat to me with such impertinence.

RAYMOND   If you find me impertinent, feel free to chastise.

SIMONE   Oh my goodness… Indefatigable, aren't we?

RAYMOND   I think you're very beautiful.

SIMONE   We've established that, what else you flogging?

RAYMOND   Iss juss that…I look at you and I do not wanna spend the rest a my life saying What If, y'get me?

SIMONE   I see…

RAYMOND   Such a precipitous balance, you don't find?

SIMONE   If you say so.

RAYMOND   I think you're very beautiful.

SIMONE   Not the first time you told me dat.

RAYMOND   I'm sorry if I've become tiresome.

SIMONE   I'll let you know when you do.

RAYMOND   Uh oh, bing bong, first chink of daylight.

SIMONE smiles.

Wow, what a smile you have…

SIMONE   I do allow myself the odd one.

RAYMOND   Been a while since I smiled too. I'm enjoying this...Dancing the dance that the dolphins dance.

SIMONE   Don't splash about too much, flipper, you might ruffle my plume.

RAYMOND   Heheh... You know what knocks me out about you? This, this...regal thing. You're a queen of the night.

SIMONE   This I will concede... You have a certain princely bearing that is not without allure...

RAYMOND   Uh, oh, bing bong, second chink a daylight.

SIMONE   Try not to see it that way, kid, you'll end up massively deflated. You're easy on the eye, toldjuh that already, don't mean nuffing, thass as far as if goes mate, and no further than that. Slow down a bit, son.

RAYMOND   Let's put the focus on you now, shall we?

SIMONE   Whafor?

RAYMOND   I find you fascinating.

SIMONE   I find you fassst.

RAYMOND   I'm, uh...I'm sensing a little bit of resistance.

SIMONE   Don't overstay your welcome, time for your horlicks.

RAYMOND   You really are laced up a little too tight, you know that? You wanna try some flotation tank, some shit like that, might help you relax your mind a little bit

SIMONE   You're boring me now, so go away.

RAYMOND   My god, you're a hard woman. I know...I know.... Some man thass made you this way, innit? Lissen sweetheart juss cause some man

ran around town getting his end away or
knocked you about a bit don't mean you and me
can't make it work, y'get me?

SIMONE   Ok. I'm a say this juss the one time…You been
moderately diverting up to now. You go any
further and you'll force me to decimate you arse.
Now. You are well out of your depth, son. I. Am.
Not. Interested. In you. No part a you. Not even
a little bit a you. Now. Go dangle somewhere
else.

RAYMOND   No, no, this is Raymond LeGendre you're
dealing with…

Song – Primus Humanus

Look me fully in the eye
Tell me you don't want me
Look me fully in the eye
Say you don't want my baby
I am the man of steel
Primus Humanus
This is it, it's all here
Don't get no better than this
Jus look me full in the eye
Say you don't want my baby

(*Rap.*) If you need a good lover, no bother
look no further
I am the man Raymond LeGendre
committing bedroom murder
Raise your blood pressure, make your
heart start beat faster
Cause when it comes to making love the
LeGendre is the master
You ask me what I'm flogging
It's just a little loving

So keep your cool, don't act the fool and
baby stop your bugging
You tell me that I'm vain
Seems to me you're in some pain
Obviously you been hurt before but every
man is not the same, juss…

(*Song.*) Look me fully in the eye
Tell me you don't want me
Look me fully in the eye
Say you don't want my baby

(*Speech over bassline.*) My body is a map of any
conceivable female desire.
It don't get any better than this.
Believe me. I'll probe you to your core. I'll set
you free. I'll make you sing, girl. I'll make you
breathe fire. I'll swim inside you on the deepest
indigo seabed. Schools of multi-coloured fish
will dart between our bodies, through your
hair…I'm a hurricane. I'm a tidal wave. I just
have to look at a woman…And she gives birth
to my child.

Look me fully in the eye
Tell me you don't want me
Look me fully in the eye
Say you don't want my baby
Look me fully in the eye
Tell me you're not wet…yet

SIMONE   Foolish boyyyy…

Song – Walk Like You Want Me

I see you walking
Round like you want me
You can talk all you like
But you can't have me

39

Cause I know you better than you know
y'self
And yes, kid, thass experience, I been out
here for a few
I been sat here lissening to your tired story
And boy, you have bored me to death
You tell me it don't get any better than you
But let me tell you something and it might
be breaking news
I'm more woman than you could ever take
I'm more woman than you could ever take
You call y'self a hurricane
But I can barely feel the breeze
So, please, please

(*Spoken over bassline.*) So where you done time?

RAYMOND   Whatchou say?

SIMONE   So where you done time?

RAYMOND   You are labouring under a dangerous
misapprehension, girl.

SIMONE   Not been out too long either, look at you,
you're in a fever, wanna getchour little cock wet
before you get banged up again, you exuuuuude
incarceration, iss in that sweat across you top lip,
it's in your wet breath, lemme tell boutchourself,
you took a long bath today, didn't you sweetboy,
cause you stunk a prison, didn't you sweetboy,
looked at yourself and kept tellin y'self...

You looked good
You look good
You look good like a casanova should
You look good
You look good
You look good like a casanova should

40

You looked good
You looked good
You look good like a casanova should
You look good
You look good
Like a little boy lost in the wood
Stood there lost in your reflection
Of sexual perfection
But I see though your shit and see your
fear
Now look me fully in the eye and tell me
that ain't you
Tell me
Tell me
Tell meeee

(*Spoken.*) Weak.
Weak.
Weak.
Laters, fool.

RAYMOND   Nah, nah, fuck that, you wait there, lemme show
you the vibe, you say you know me, you don't
know fuckall about me right. You say you know
me but what could you know about a man like
me and my kinda pedigree? You claiming you
can look past my mask, but you ain't even close.
I been flushed down a toilet and forced to make
my home in a sewer for three years. Three years
a my life that ain't ever coming back, three years
counting bricks in a wall. And watch how them
visiting times get thin as your friends can't face
looking at you and how changed. Watch how
you become a ghost to your own heart. Watch
how regret come and bite your face. Watch
how you dyin inside. I ain't seen the moon rise
nor the sun set for one thousand ninety five
days. And since they let me out all I can do is

41

prowling and pacing and clenchin my teeth til
I get the courage up to let myself out my own
place steada watchin the car headlights sweeping
past the ceiling all night. Been dreamin 'bout
stepping out and beguliing the night time like I
used to, reclaimin whass mine and the first time
I got out the door is tonight.
Yeah.
You think I need to be taken down a peg or two.
I thank you for your concern.

RAYMOND makes to exit.

SIMONE   Wait.

RAYMOND   Whafor, so you can reload?

SIMONE   Yeah, well, I'm sorry.

RAYMOND   Yeah, well, laters.

SIMONE   Wait.

RAYMOND reluctantly stops.

I saw, uh…I saw my little girl at the weekend…
Buttoning up her coat and she looked at me
plain soldier and said 'You're a young lady. And
there ARE monsters out there, but you have to
go out anyway'. She's three years old.

RAYMOND   Thass nice. Gotta go.

SIMONE   Wait.

RAYMOND stops.

You got any kids?

Pause.

RAYMOND   Some.

Pause.

SIMONE   Ok then… Fair enough… See you.

            Pause.

RAYMOND   Ain't quite finished my drink yet.

            Pause.

            So whass your li'l girl's name?

SIMONE   Mandy.

RAYMOND   S'a nice name.

SIMONE   Yeah. She fell down the other day when we was
            running for a bus. Juss a scratch and a scrape,
            but you shoulda heard how she howled.

            Pause.

RAYMOND   Public transport's terrible these days.

            Pause.

SIMONE   What did you do, Raymond?

            Pause.

RAYMOND   I was stupid. I wasn't violent. Juss two wrong
            turns and I was IN. End of.

SIMONE   You sure?

RAYMOND   Positive.

SIMONE   You telling me the truth now?

RAYMOND   May god gimme herpes if I lie.

SIMONE   Boy, I hope it don't come to that.

            Pause.

            You're a goodlooking guy, you know that,
            Raymond?

            Enter YVONNE.

YVONNE   Jake's is booming over there.

SIMONE   Whass the rations like?

YVONNE   A number of attractive offers. You ready to go?

SIMONE   Come on then.

RAYMOND   Stay a little.

SIMONE   I'm going with my mate.

RAYMOND   Uh…You on the phone?

SIMONE   Yes thanks.

RAYMOND   Can I have your number?

SIMONE   You gimme yours.

RAYMOND scribbles down his number on a matchbook.

RAYMOND   S'my mobile.

SIMONE   Thanks.

RAYMOND   I'll see you.

SIMONE   I'll see you.

RAYMOND   You gonna ring me?

SIMONE   I'm gonna ring you.

RAYMOND   I'll see you.

SIMONE   I'll see you.

RAYMOND   Ring me, yeah?

SIMONE   I'm gonna.

RAYMOND   I'll see you.

SIMONE   I'll see you.

RAYMOND   Ring me.

SIMONE and YVONNE exit.

Song – Fire

There's a fire
Deep inside me
I don't wanna put out the flames
Walkin a high-wire
Above the city
Don't know the rules of this dangerous
game
What's this feeling
That I'm feeling?
Feeling like I'm born again
From the moment that I saw her
I knew I'd never feel the same
(She's gonna burn ya
The girl's gonna burn ya
She's gonna burn ya
Burn your heart)
This woman's got me in a tailspin
And I'm not able to pull out
Looks like I'm crash and burn
Pull the wreckage out my heart
Those eyes of hers bewitch me
They spellbind and confuse me
Don't know which way is up or down
That voice of hers like honey
Flows warmly flowin smoothly
Don't wanna hear no other sound
Now I'm hopin for a future
Forgettin all that's in my past
I've been searching Lonely hunter
She turns it all to smoke and ash
Those eyes of hers bewitch me

They dazzle me, confuse me
Don't know which way is up or down
That voice of hers like honey
Flows warmly flowin smoothly
Don't wanna hear no other sound
I just can't go on
Without her in my arms
There's a fire deep inside me

(She's gonna burn ya,
The girl's gonna burn ya
She's gonna burn your heart)

SIMONE re-enters.

End Act One.

Act Two

One week later.

BARNEY polishing glasses.

Song – Rivers

BARNEY   I'm crying rivers
So not much has changed
But if she cried with me
Then I'd never cry again
I'm on my way out
For the last time
I'm tired of holding on
Juss gonna let go
Start to sink
Start to sink
I'm crying rivers
And that's alright
But if she cried with me
Then I'll make it through the night
I'll be stronger than I've ever been before
Holding on for the last time
And this is my last shot
Please come home with me
Please come home with me
Please come home with me *(x5 til fade.)*

Enter SIMONE, furious.

SIMONE   Where is he? Where is that asshole?

BARNEY   Simone?

SIMONE   Gonna find him and stab him!

BARNEY   Take a drink. Slow down.

BARNEY pours her a drink.

SIMONE   I'll do him. I'll do him.

BARNEY   Simone… Who you gonna do?

SIMONE   Mandy's dad.

BARNEY   Whasshe doneya?

SIMONE takes out her phone and dials.

Simone… Who you calling?

SIMONE   My cousin. Shoulda got him to do this a long time ago. Make Mandy's dad die.

BARNEY   Simone. Simone. Simone. Drink your drink. Just drink. Listen to me. Wait and listen. If you call your cousin, it get out of control. Game over. Carnage and chaos. You don't want that.

SIMONE drains off her drink.

SIMONE   Lemme distress a next drink.

BARNEY pours another. She drains it in one.

BARNEY   Better?

SIMONE   More.

BARNEY pours her another.

Ah. There. Click. Better.

BARNEY   Whass the apple? I got time.

SIMONE   Li'l fucker's been seeing my kid. I know he has. I gotta keep her away from his sickness. Got to kill him.

BARNEY   All this violent talk... I never even seen you
            make a fist.

SIMONE   Wanna know whatchour trouble is, Barn?
            Lemme tell you whatchour trouble is. Lemme
            tell you, article and bonafide. You don't have the
            courage of your convictions. Thass it. Plain and
            simple. You gotta take risks in this rough ocean.
            You too scared. Behind that bar. Peering in at it
            all, not splashing about with rest of us. You're
            missing out, mate. Lemme tell you... You Gets
            No Guarantees.

BARNEY   You Gets No Guarantees.

SIMONE   S'right. Whadjuh think a that?

BARNEY   Tablets of wisdom from the mountain top, thass
            what I think of that.

SIMONE   Seize that moment, B. Wrestle with it. Wring it
            dry.

BARNEY   I'll try and do that.

            Pause.

SIMONE   Do you think I'm a nice person, B? Do you
            think I'm an ok type of bird?

BARNEY   I think you're a wonderful typa bird.

SIMONE   You're sweet.

BARNEY   Thank you.

SIMONE   Wanna putchou in my pocket, B.

BARNEY   I'm touched.

            SIMONE is pretty drunk.

            She rests her head on the counter and quietly sobs.
            BARNEY watches, paralysed.

He reaches out to caress her hair, but before he can make a contact...YVONNE enters.

BARNEY withdraws his hand. No-one notices.

BARNEY withdraws.

YVONNE   Simone, where you been? I knocked round your mum's, she said you ain't been there, Mandy wants to know where you got to and all.

SIMONE   (*Sobs.*) I'm a bad motherrrrr…

YVONNE   How much she had to drink, B?

BARNEY   Enough.

YVONNE   Simone, what's happened to you? I ain't seen you like this, whass wrong, girl?

SIMONE   I'm fine.

YVONNE   You're a state.

SIMONE   I said I'm fine.

YVONNE   Oy, this is me, remember. Known you from time.

SIMONE   Get off me, Yvonne.

YVONNE   I held your hand when you give birth.

SIMONE   I'm fine.

YVONNE   You know I love you like cook food, Simone. Whass the apple?

SIMONE   Oh god… You remember that guy that was in here last night?

YVONNE   From when we last in here? The skinny runty fella? I just pass that braer on the road talkin 'bout 'the hour of vengeance is at hand! I sense him! I sense him near! I sense him!' All up and down the high street.

SIMONE   Not the one looking for a fight, the one looking for a fuck.

YVONNE   Yeah. Raymond. Raymond summink.

SIMONE   Raymond LeGendre.

YVONNE   What about him?

SIMONE   Oh god...

YVONNE   Tell me! I'll hit you, you know.

SIMONE   I'll hit you back, you know.

YVONNE   I'll slap you in the mouth with one a my tits, you don't tell me the apple.

SIMONE laughs.

Thass better. Whass this geeza do? My cut-throat is at the ready.

SIMONE   I...I...I...I went to bed with him.

Pause.

YVONNE   Is that all?

SIMONE nods her head, yes.

Well, what, did he...did he take a shit on you or summink?

SIMONE shakes her head no.

Well, whass the problem? Lousy lay? Nine men outta ten, I'm afraid, darling.

SIMONE   I found his number on a matchbook and 'bout to dash it when I remembered something I seen in his eyes and I called him up and he was so excited he couldn't hide it we met up and jokes and laughs and gentleness and a thrill to it, a dazzle in my belly when I look in his eyes and I'm thinking, I'm thinking this guy really has

something, a sweetness, a weight, we're watching
the sky burnish purple red, and we watched
each other watched each other a lot and my
belly's getting dazzled and then we kissed, but
he didn't kiss me like ordinary blokes kiss me,
he kissed ME, y'know? He kissed my entire
history, y'understand? Kissed my history. He
anointed me.

Song – Thunder and Gold

The evening just flowed
The whole night just flowed – we took it
Mellow and slow
Fashioned from thunder
And chiselled with gold
Gold
Car headlights sweeping cross the ceiling,
My heart is reeling.
Do you feel my heart beating?

It's funny how you can feel so lonely and
never know it
It's funny how you can want to cry and
never show it

He touched me and took me
This feeling I don't understand,
My heart is breaking in his hand.

I don't know if this is gonna be something
lasting
Or if it's just another one night flex.
We were just two hearts dancing
And I don't know what's coming next

He touched me and took me
This feeling I don't understand,
My heart is breaking in his hand

And now I don't know who I am.

End song.

YVONNE   And?

SIMONE   And now I know what the fuck you been going on about all these years ! Now I know my own strength. Raymond tapped me into my own strength.

YVONNE   Sounds alright.

SIMONE   Yes.

YVONNE   So when you checking him again?

SIMONE sobs.

Oh shit, Simone… He blanked you, didn't he? Got what he wanted and give you your P45… I'll kill him for you.

SIMONE   No, he begged me to stay, then he begged for my number, then he begged me to call him again.

YVONNE   So you fucked his brains out and you ain't call him?

SIMONE nods yes.

Thass a style. That is a fuckin style. Simone, you learn.

SIMONE sobs.

So whatchou blubbing for?

SIMONE   I…I wanna see him…

YVONNE   So call him why doncha?

SIMONE   No. No. Never. Learnt my lesson with Mandy's dad Never surrender, never concede, never forgive.

YVONNE   This Raymond geeza ain't Mandy's dad, you
          dodo.

SIMONE   He is. They all are. They juss come in a different
          wrapping.

YVONNE   What happened with Mandy's dad was
          unfortunate, but life spins on and we're meant to
          live the bastard, y'get me?

SIMONE   Unfortunate? Unfortunate? Mandy's dad told
          me when I was pregnant, get rid of that shit in
          your stomach, and when she was born disabled
          he told me it couldn't be his kid, said no kid of
          his could come out so half-finished. That's what
          we made together. I Let him grow inside me.

YVONNE   Mandy is a beautiful child who's blessed all our
          lives.

SIMONE   Mandy's seen her dad somehow, Yvonne,
          thrown a big fit about how she wants to see him.
          He's got to her somehow, but I dunno how.

YVONNE   Lissen, Simone… Don't go on stink alright?
          Lissen… Remember I took care of Mandy on
          my day off, took her down the swings? Well…
          Look…he was there… Can of kestrel in his
          hand. Simone? Simone, I didn't know what to
          do… That is his daughter… He was in love with
          the whole thing… 'She's grown so big' he says…
          What was I… Don't hate me, Simone… We
          went to his place, not for long, juss long enough
          to drink a cup of tea… Don't… Simone… I
          think he's really changed… We all change,
          Simone…

          Song – Anyone Can Change

          Anyone can change, sometimes for the
          better, Simone

And life spins onwards
We're moving on so fast but I'm sticking
by you – Simone
Life gets harder but life gets sweeter
Harsh times we been through have turned
you hard
Unfreeze your heart, let down your
guard – Simone
Even you can change
You can change for the better – Simone
Cause nothing's set in stone

End song.

I'll slap in the mouth with one of my tits…

SIMONE has turned to stone.

YVONNE exits in silence.

SIMONE   I am no longer drunk.

BARNEY hands her a drink.

You don't say a whole lot, do you Barney?

BARNEY   Summink you wanna hear me say?

SIMONE   Yeah.

BARNEY   What?

SIMONE   Say 'You're strong enough to put it behind you.'

BARNEY   Juss that?

SIMONE   Yes, please.

BARNEY   You're strong enough to put it behind you.

SIMONE   Do you really think so? Now you say that
you do.

BARNEY   I do.

SIMONE   Thank you.

BARNEY   You're welcome.

She drains her drink.

Song – If this is the Truth

BARNEY   (*Sings*) I've stopped breathing since I saw you

And my heart would break if you saw me now

So I'll…stay here in the dark

SIMONE   Everything's changin oh so fast

BARNEY   Don't know where to start

SIMONE   …and I know there's no turning back

SIMONE AND BARNEY

If this is the truth

Then the truth hurts more than you will ever know

If this is the truth

Then the truth hurts more than you'll ever know

BARNEY   I've tried so hard to give you my heart

But all I give is closed eyes and silence

SIMONE   I don't

No I don't know

I don't know I don't know I don't know what I want

SIMONE AND BARNEY

If this is the truth

Then the truth hurts

BARNEY   There's a light around you

There's a light around you

> There's a light around you
> There's a light around you
> And it's not going out
> It's not going out
> It's not going out
> It's not going out

SIMONE
> What if he hurts me
> What if I lose my way again
> Everything's changed now
> And I'm not the same
> Cause he's all that I need
> Yeah, he's all that I want
> Raymond there's a light around you
> Raymond there's a light around you

BARNEY   This is the truth that you will never know

SIMONE
> But your light's too bright
> I'm gonna get burned
> Gonna get burned again
> So I'm gonna find the dark

Song ends.

SIMONE heads for the door.

BARNEY   Simone?

SIMONE   Yes, B?

BARNEY   Don't matter.

Pause.

SIMONE   Whatchou got on your mind?

BARNEY   All sorts.

SIMONE   You seen him around recently, Barney?

Pause.

BARNEY	I heard he got a girl out in Willesden.
	Pause.
SIMONE	You ever been in love?
BARNEY	Only with you, Simone.
SIMONE	Hehehe. You silver-tongued so and so, you.
	SIMONE exits.
	BARNEY pours a whisky into a glass.
BARNEY	You can come out now, Raymond.
	RAYMOND emerges from the men's toilets. He picks up his drink.
	You hear all that?
RAYMOND	I never begged her for her numba. I never begged her for nuffink.
BARNEY	Whatchou gonna do about her, Raymond?
RAYMOND	Them toilets stink.
BARNEY	Whatchou gonna do about her?
	Pause.
	You still checkin that girl from Willesden?
RAYMOND	Whatchou tell her about that for?
BARNEY	She asked me. I ain't gonna lie to her.
RAYMOND	Bollox.
BARNEY	You still checkin her ?
RAYMOND	Yeah, I'm still checkin her.
BARNEY	She got a geezer, y'know.
RAYMOND	Ain't no sweeter feeling grinding a next man's missus.

58

BARNEY   Y'know something, Raymond? You juss
            perpretatin a façade on y'self. Stop livin a lie.

RAYMOND   Shut up. You ain't even got the belly to talk
            to a woman, much less tell 'em how you felt.
            Name me one time, name me one time when
            you swam so deep your feet couldn't touch the
            seabed.

            Pause.

            The phone rings.

            BARNEY answers it.

BARNEY   Hello, Bar Phoenix... Hello, Jake, how
            y'doing?...ha Ha...uh huh...I'll tell you what,
            I'll swap you some ice for some of my customers
            back...ha hah... I'll be right over.

RAYMOND   (*Overlapping with BARNEY.*) Eunuch in a harem...
            raincoat nonce...voyeur...vampire...

BARNEY   Jake's need to borrow some ice, can I trust you
            to run the bar for a few minutes?

RAYMOND   Why can't Jake come and get it hisself if he
            needs sumink from you?

BARNEY   I need to speak to Jake.

RAYMOND   Tryna get a job over there when this gaff shuts
            down?

BARNEY   Don't touch the booze while I'm gone, alright?

RAYMOND   I won't touch the booze, what, you think I'm a
            child?

            BARNEY exits with a sack of ice.

            *As soon as he's gone, RAYMOND pours himself a
            brandy.*

RAYMOND   What is he, my mother? Don't recall suckin milk from those titties.

RAYMOND drains his drink in one.

Ahhh… Finished…shit…

RAYMOND slumps in his chair.

GIL sneaks into the bar, knife in hand.

RAYMOND, in a world of his own, does not sense him.

GIL grabs him and holds a knife to his throat.

Oh hello.

GIL   Be still.

Pause.

How are you, Raymond LeGendre?

RAYMOND   Uh… Little stressed…suddenly quite sober… How are you?

GIL   Shut up.

RAYMOND   Fine.

Pause.

GIL   Y'looking as dapper as ever.

RAYMOND   Thank you.

GIL   Pretty as a picture.

RAYMOND   How comes you know my name?

GIL   Hehehehe… Ah well now, y'know…

RAYMOND   You're not here to rob this gaff, are you?

GIL   No, I'm not.

RAYMOND   You're here for me.

GIL   Yes.

RAYMOND   You've come to cut me.

GIL   Yes.

RAYMOND   You've come to kill me.

GIL   Yes, I have.

RAYMOND   I don't even know you and you've come to kill me. You getting paid? Who hates me? What have I done him?

GIL   You do know me, Raymond LeGendre.

RAYMOND   Where? Where from?

GIL   I've waited so long to have you in this position.

RAYMOND   What have I done you?

GIL   I almost don't know what to do with you, I'm so pleased with myself.

RAYMOND   Be reasonable, eh? Whass all this about?

GIL   Wondering whass the best way to prolong your suffering, get my full three year's worth.

RAYMOND   There must be a way we can –

GIL   Could slice your nipples off.

RAYMOND   Come on, mate.

GIL   Stick a pencil in your ear, kick it into your brain.

RAYMOND   Please, mate.

GIL   Maybe decorate your face before I kill you.

RAYMOND   De.de.de.de.decorate my face?

GIL   Paint pretty pictures on it.

RAYMOND   My face?

GIL   Yes, ruin your face.

RAYMOND   Not my face, not my face, not my face.

GIL   I reckon thass favourite

RAYMOND   I don't even know you!

GIL   You do know me.

RAYMOND   You're so young. What did I do to make you
               wanna hurt me so much?

GIL   You took my girl.

RAYMOND   Do what?

GIL   You Took My Girl.

RAYMOND   Hold on mate... I got a certain reputation for
               things, not entirely unmerited, iss true, but a lot
               of it juss jealous people spreading rumours about
               me and really iss juss folklore, y'know mate?
               S'juss folklore.

GIL   You took my girl from me right in front of my
               face.

RAYMOND   Shit.

GIL   In my face.

RAYMOND   I swear I didn't know she was your girl.

GIL   Don't make no difference.

RAYMOND   I'm sorry.

GIL   You gutted me. We was gonna be so happy
               together.

RAYMOND   You sure it was me?

GIL   Yes, I'm sure it was you, you think I'd go to
               these fuckin lengths if I wasn't sure? What am I,
               a fuckin prat?

RAYMOND   Whass her name, this girl?

Pause.

Mate? What was her name?

GIL   Enjoyable, was it? Putting your hands all over
my missus? Fuck her brains out? Left her
dripping?

RAYMOND   Mate, please...try not think about that... Tell me
about her. Who was she? I wanna know about
her.

Pause.

GIL   I first met her on July twenny ninth, 2003.

RAYMOND   Thass over three years ago.

GIL   Hot day, roastingly hot day, in the nineties if
not the hundreds. Hadn't been awake that long,
juss enough to scratch my arse, smoke a spliff
and hear the radio weatherman say 'fuck me,
it's hot out there'. Heard my girocheque slap
the lino, and thought, I'd go post office. Didn't
wash, didn't shave, didn't even brush my teeth.
I thought, I'm only going post office. Wore these
stupid foul smelling black trainers big rip down
the side toes poking out. No socks. I was not
looking good. Cash my giro at the post office,
counting out my sheks... SHE walks in. She was
so beautiful, I got a nosebleed juss from looking
at her. She was perfect. She was an angel. I got
blood bubblin' out my shnozz, onto my chin,
all over my shirt, my ripped up trainers. Sweat
flowing from my armpits. She comes past,
gliding past my blood on the floor.

This magical magical magical magical magical
woman.

When I tell you this girl was fire... She clickety claxed past me and out into the heat. I thought, I thought, 'fuck it, I'm following her', I thought. Step out behind her, watchin that backside syncopating. She's doing it on purpose, right? She's doing it for me. So now it's crunch time, I have to chirps her, chirps her the best I know how, I'm gearing meself up for it...I draw level, and she...she...

Song – Smile

She smiled this smile
And I melted down to the floor
Kinda smile
That I've never seen before
She smiled
And I coulda died
I never knew I'd see an angel
I didn't wanna squander the chance
A perfect angel
How my heart moved to dance
And ever since that fateful day
I'm in love
I'm in love
I'm in love
And it won't go awaaaaayyyy

(*Spoken.*) So I think, fuck it Gil, you've come this far, turn round and lyrics her, don't be a loser all your life. So I take a huge deep breath and turn around... And there you was... You looked like a, like a world class athlete. You looked so beautiful... Crisp cream shorts stop just above the knee. Tachini tennis shirt. Then the piece de fuckin resistance, a pair of old school julius erving Dr J trainers look fresh out the fuckin box. Do you play tennis? Do you play basketball? Where the fuck did you find a pair of old school julius erving Dr J Trainers? All the appeal, all the right feel. Charisma to burn. I watch you spellbind my woman in front a me. Then you got in her motor and sped off. I fuckin stood there, rank as fuck, sweating and squintin. I thought, I thought... 'Fuck me', I thought. What a sense of loss. Inconsolable loss. You shat on me, Raymond LeGendre. And thass why you have to die.

Pause.

RAYMOND   Does it make a difference that I can't remember her?

GIL lights up a big spliff.

GIL   I'm gonna cut you til I can't see you. And when I can't see you, I'm gonna cut where you was.

RAYMOND   Gimme a pull on that spliff, please, seeing as I'm about to die.

GIL passes him the joint.

GIL   Juss one question, Raymond LeGendre. Did her skin smell nice? It's the one thing I can't imagine. She looked like she smelled nice. Like burnt sugar.

RAYMOND   I can't place this bird, can't place her at all. I'm gonna die over a bird you never had, and I can't remember.

GIL   She make nice noises?

RAYMOND   Mate, if I could remember, I'd act the whole thing out for you, but I'm telling you, she's lost in the pageant of history.

GIL   In my head, she's very tender and slow.

RAYMOND   You really are hooked... You got it bad, kid.

GIL You don't know… You don't know…

RAYMOND I'm sorry.

GIL You don't know what love is. To wake up and see her face on the ceiling.

RAYMOND To talk to her, even though she's not there.

GIL To daily feel the wrench, the physical wrench of being apart from her.

RAYMOND And it is physical. The pain is physical. Like being ill.

GIL Want her to touch you so bad…

RAYMOND Any other touch feels like a stab.

GIL To spend days pleading with yourself to banish her from your brain.

RAYMOND But still she comes, like a thief in the night.

GIL Eating your mind.

RAYMOND The slightest breeze brings her perfume to your nose.

GIL Keep thinking you see her. In the park, in the shops

RAYMOND In your sheets…

GIL To have a woman's flavour misting up your mind…

RAYMOND To feel your heart burst with tenderness…

GIL My love for her is mystical…

RAYMOND Lyrical…

GIL Metaphysical…

RAYMOND Yes…

GIL   (*Bites back tears.*) You don't know what love is…
                You don't know… You've got no inkling…She's
                so beautiful… So beautiful…

                *GIL sags into RAYMOND's arms. RAYMOND cradles
                him, spliff in mouth.*

RAYMOND   It's hell, isn't it? Pure hell.

                BARNEY enters.

                He takes in the scene.

BARNEY   Jake's is packed over there.

                *GIL takes RAYMOND's hand and places it on his
                head.*

GIL   Stroke my hair like how mum did when I was a
                kid.

RAYMOND   I'm in it with you, mate. I'm in that same space.

BARNEY   Whass happened to the brandy, Raymond?

RAYMOND   Ssshhh. He's Just going off.

                GIL is asleep in RAYMOND's arms.

                *RAYMOND carries him and gently places him on a
                low sofa.*

                You ever see this kid before?

BARNEY   No.

RAYMOND   He's in love.

                Enter YVONNE, very drunk.

YVONNE   Who the fuck does Jake think he is, what kinda
                poxy shithole does he wanna attach his name to,
                gaff's got no class, no fuckin class at all, not even
                a whiff of it, him and his rancid little drinking
                hole forgetting who makes camden, it ain't the
                fuckin MTV bods, the fuckin boho tourists,

it's the fuckin residents, the ones who have
to walk street when the market done and the
pavement heave with takeways, cartons and old
newspaper, and him across the road exasperates
the problem because he's quite content to fill his
bar with goateed fools and overpainted spandex
trollops sitting round waiting to get fucked so
they got summink to talk about when they at
whatever work it is these nightmare scabby
tarts actually do, that joint is crusty as fuck, it
don't have a smidgeon of style or pizzazz or
authenticness and the one thing it cate-fuckin-
gorically is not in possession of is the indefinable
thing which we call CLASS.

Pause.

(*To BARNEY.*) I wanna fuck you.

BARNEY	The usual?
YVONNE	Where the fuck's everybody got to?
BARNEY	Jake's.
YVONNE	I had this dream about a bloke with a dick for a tongue.
RAYMOND	Yvonne…donchou think you should go home to bed?
YVONNE	Was I talking to you, no I wasn't talking to you, because I don't talk to watless eeedyats who think they're pretty, so jus hold your space and be quiet. (*To BARNEY.*) I want to fuck you.

GIL wakes with a start.

GIL	S'ok, Luke, I'll drive.
YVONNE	Look, it's the lairy prat from last night.
GIL	Who let the slapper in?

RAYMOND   Do summink, Barney.

           RAYMOND's mobile phone rings.

BARNEY   Just answer your phone, Raymond.

YVONNE   Fuck off, call me a slapper, you flaccid nonce, I'll
           kill ya.

BARNEY   Don't kick it off on the last night of the bar.

GIL   You can go fuck y'self for a start, love.

YVONNE   Bollocks.

RAYMOND   (*Into phone.*) H'llo? Oh. Yeah. Where's your
           husband?

GIL   I ain't got an husband

RAYMOND   You want me to come to Willesden now?

BARNEY   Fellas, please. A little class, eh?

YVONNE   Who arxed you to talk? 'Bout class.

RAYMOND   Well…you got a husband, love.

BARNEY   Who's having what?

RAYMOND   Well, I don't think I'm that sort of geeza…

GIL   Fuck you, you tart.

YVONNE   Fuck you with bells on, needle-knob.

RAYMOND   I know it didn't bother me before, but…

GIL   Tart.

YVONNE   Wanker.

GIL   Slag.

YVONNE   Virgin.

BARNEY   Can I get anyone a drink?

YVONNE Wine, wine, I must worship bacchus, t'bleemos.

RAYMOND He's your husband, love, thass gotta mean summink.

GIL I'll have a fanta, please, skipper.

RAYMOND Well, I mean…doncha love him?

YVONNE I had this dream about a bloke with a cock for a tongue the other night.

BARNEY House white do you?

RAYMOND Well, I think it matters…

GIL Could he actually speak with it?

YVONNE Only in fucked tongues, hahahaha.

YVONNE and GIL crack up laughing.

BARNEY Thass what I like to hear, a happy bar.

GIL Fucked tongues, thass a funny one.

YVONNE Course iss funny, I said it.

GIL Flash tart.

YVONNE Silly fool.

RAYMOND WHY THE FUCK ARE YOU MAKING THIS SO DIFFICULT! I don't wanna see you, I don't feel right about, I WANNA BE AN ADULT!

RAYMOND hangs up.

BARNEY Everything alright, Raymond?

RAYMOND What have I just done? I never turned down a grind in my life.

BARNEY Probly for the best, Raymond.

RAYMOND I'm sorry, Barney. 'Bout before. 'Bout calling you a voyeur.

BARNEY   Forget it. I have.

BARNEY takes the drinks over to GIL and YVONNE.

Here we are.

GIL   Ah, thanks, mate.

YVONNE   You ever accuse me of havin no class again, I'll spit in your eyeball.

BARNEY   I'll try and remember.

GIL   Easy, love. Barney's my mate. Been like a father to me.

YVONNE   You're sweet.

GIL   No, I'm not. I'm sour. Hahhahahahahahahahahahaha

YVONNE   Let's have a party! Dead in here.

GIL   Let's wreck things.

YVONNE   Let's dance.

GIL jumps up and grabs YVONNE by the waist.

Song – This is What You Want

(*Spoken.*) Dance wimme, Gil, you bony malnourished fractured psychopathic manchild, you!

GIL   (*Spoken.*) Hold on tight, you clapped out crabby old slapper! HERE WE GO!

They are both spinning round relentlessly.

(*Sung.*) This is what you want, isn't it?
This is what you want
Isn't it
This is what you want

71

Isn't it
This is what you want
I'm gonna give you what you want
I'm gonna give you what you want
This is what you want
I'm gonna spin you round like this forever,
You ain't met no-one like me and you shall
never so come on,
Come on,
Come ooooooooowwwwwnnnn
Yooowwwww

SIMONE enters. She sees GIL spinning YVONNE round, hears him shouting at her and misreads the situation.

She grabs a beer bottle and smashes it over GIL's head.

SIMONE   Fuckin leave my friend alone, shithead!

GIL crashes to the floor, releasing YVONNE, who spins into a table, knocking it to the floor.

BARNEY   Last night of the bar and I gotta put up with this!

SIMONE   Yvonne? You alright? He hurt you?

YVONNE   Gil! Gil! You've hurt Gil!

SIMONE   What?

YVONNE   Wake him up! Do summink!

BARNEY   Alright, alright.

SIMONE   Have I distressed the sesh?

RAYMOND cradles the unconscious GIL.

RAYMOND   Got any smelling salts?

SIMONE   Stuck my foot in it, haven't I, babes?

BARNEY   Smelling salts? Think this is a war flick or
            summink?

YVONNE   Whachou come back here for anyways?

RAYMOND   Wake up, Gil !

SIMONE   Don't be like that, Yvonne.

YVONNE   You juss laced my comrade!

BARNEY   Dash a drop of brandy down his gob.

SIMONE   I'm sorry, darling, but last time you saw him you
            had a cut-throat on him, I can't keep up with
            your lovelife as it is.

YVONNE   People change, Simone, thass all I'm sayin.

            *RAYMOND splashes brandy in GIL's mouth GIL
            splutters but does not wake.*

RAYMOND   Well, if you don't want it...

            RAYMOND takes a mighty swig from the bottle.

SIMONE   I know people change, thass why I come back
            here tonight.

BARNEY   Raymond, will you stop drinking the stock? We
            have a perilous situation here.

SIMONE   I'm sorry I went on stink before, Yvonne. Really
            and truly.

RAYMOND   I need to steady my hand, in case I need to
            operate.

YVONNE   It ain't easy being your friend, y'know.

            BARNEY slaps GIL.

BARNEY   Gilly, Gilly, come on, up you get, my little
            chipolata.

SIMONE   I know it ain't but I've learnt a lot from you
          tonight.

RAYMOND   He is fuckin sparko.

SIMONE   I don't wanna be such a hard-faced cow the rest
          a my life, I wana bend a little.

YVONNE   So whatchou sayin?

RAYMOND   He looks kinda peaceful, really, like a little
          cherub.

SIMONE   I'm saying do you still wanna be my mate,
          because I still want you to be my mate.

BARNEY   He does, rather.

YVONNE   Well, now...

SIMONE   Tell me! I'll hit you, y'know.

YVONNE   I'll hit you back, y'know.

SIMONE   I'll smack you in the mouth with one a my tits, if
          you don't be my friend no more.

YVONNE   Well, I wouldn't want that, now would I? Not
          with those tits.

          The girls embrace.

BARNEY   We really do need to get this guy awake.

YVONNE   (*Overlapping with SIMONE.*) Oh god, Simone
          I just, I'm sorry I messed up with your kid, I
          shoulda thought ahead, thass my trouble really, I
          wasn't thinking about the followthrough –

SIMONE   (*Overlapping with above.*) No baby iss all me being
          unforgiving, Mandy has gotta know who her
          dad is, I know that really, I juss got a blind spot
          about all that, I let my stupid pride get away
          from me –

74

YVONNE (*Bites back tears.*) Y'not unforgiving, you're a wonderful person and a sensitive mother.

BARNEY Reckon we need an ambulance.

SIMONE Yvonne, darling, let's you and me never have another row ever.

YVONNE Never, and let's you and me never be apart for a single day.

SIMONE Easy now love, steady on.

RAYMOND Aha! I have the solution!

RAYMOND picks up the half-smoked spliff from the ashtray.

BARNEY Raymond... Gettin stoned is never the solution.

RAYMOND Silence! Observez vous!

RAYMOND lights and the spiff and blows the smoke into GIL's face.

GIL immediately sits bolt upright.

GIL I'll have a one-day travelcard zones and two, please.

RAYMOND AND BARNEY Yes!

YVONNE Y'alright, Gil, mate?

GIL I was dancing with some gorgeous bird, and then –

SIMONE I laced you. Heh. Sorry. Misconstrued that shit.

GIL You're safe, love.

BARNEY It was Raymond's quick thinking that saved you.

GIL Raymond, you are a river to your people.

BARNEY What a shithole.

YVONNE   How you doing?

GIL   Pretty good, actually, juss wanna lay down and catch two zzzz.

         GIL lies down on the sofa and falls asleep instantly.

BARNEY   Do what you want, but don't make no mess for others to clean up, thass my philosophy.

SIMONE   Yvonne?

YVONNE   Yes, babes?

SIMONE   You my friend?

YVONNE   You know it, honey.

SIMONE   Go away for a little while.

YVONNE   Oh.

         Pause.

         You want my advice, run a mile. He's a pussy.

SIMONE   Thanks. Go away.

         YVONNE exits.

         BARNEY senses the mood and exits.

         Hello.

RAYMOND Hello.

SIMONE   It's… Don't tell me… It's Raymond, isn't it?

RAYMOND Wanna drink?

SIMONE   You buyin?

         RAYMOND pours two drinks.

         How's tricks?

RAYMOND Tricks are good.

SIMONE   Good.

RAYMOND   How's things with you?

SIMONE   Things with me are fine.

RAYMOND   I'm glad.

SIMONE   Good.

RAYMOND   Good.

           Pause.

           Lissen, I uh… Simone, I –

SIMONE   Don't worry 'self, Raymond, I ain't here to make
           no play for you, I juss stepped in looking for my
           spar.

RAYMOND   Okay.

SIMONE   Not a big thing to me at all, iss a minor, happens
           every day, I'm a big girl can buckle my own
           shoe.

RAYMOND   I getcha.

SIMONE   Iss not a deal. Movin on.

RAYMOND   Okay.

SIMONE   Good.

RAYMOND   Yes.

SIMONE   Glad we're on the same page with this.

RAYMOND   Yeah.

           Pause.

SIMONE   So there it is.

RAYMOND   If thass what time it is, thass what time it is.

SIMONE   Iss for the best.

RAYMOND   I agree.

SIMONE   Well, fine.

RAYMOND   Well, fine.

SIMONE   Best be dusting.

RAYMOND   Okay.

Pause.

SIMONE   Ain't quite finished my drink yet.

RAYMOND   Have a next one.

SIMONE   Nah. Gotta go.

SIMONE kills her drink and makes to leave.

RAYMOND   Wait.

SIMONE stops and turns back.

I, uh…I had a fantastic time the other night.

SIMONE   And?

RAYMOND   Well, I uh…I kinda think you had a fantastic time and all.

SIMONE   I'm not saying I didn't, but so what if I did?

RAYMOND   Ah. Hm. My mistake. Forget it. If it didn't mean what I thought it meant, then it meant nothing at all.

SIMONE   What meant it to you, Raymond?

Pause.

RAYMOND   I surrendered.

SIMONE   Yes.

RAYMOND   Lay down my burden, y'know? Lay down my burden.

SIMONE   I know you did.

RAYMOND   I felt so fee.

SIMONE   Yes.

RAYMOND   And complete.

SIMONE   Yes. (*Beat.*) Raymond... Don't let this go to your head, alright? I'm only gonna say this the one time. We created a universe that night.

                    Song – Universe of Love

RAYMOND   When we got together
              When we took off our masks and revealed
              We took to the sky
              The rain and thunder
              Washed all the pain away
              In our universe of love

SIMONE   Yes, you set me free
              Set me free from all the hurt
              And yes we gave each other wings
              To dance among the clouds
              And we drank from the sweet rain

RAYMOND   In our Universe Of Love

SIMONE   Universe Of Love

RAYMOND   We got a magic vibe between us
              Can't tell when you end and I begin
              Take my hand on this adventure
              And we can flow like rivers to the sea

SIMONE   Each time I blink I'm back there with you
              You burnin into my mind
              You kiss me with such liberation
              Like a shooting star across my heart

> You say that you want me
> But I'm not just a runaround girl
> You say that you need me
> But I'm not here just to grind me and leave
> me

RAYMOND   Simone I know you don't wanna believe
            me
            But look in my eyes and see
            I'm the real deal girl, and this is the truth
            That your heart is safe with me

SIMONE   Don't try to deceive me
            I'm not here to be made a fool of

RAYMOND   Baby don't leave me

SIMONE   Stop messin with my heeead

RAYMOND   I'm not messin you just gotta trust me

SIMONE   Raymond, don't hurt me

RAYMOND   Simone, I won't hurt you

SIMONE   You got such a sweetness

RAYMOND   You got such a sweetness

SIMONE   I'm drownin
            I'm fallin

Pause.

No. No, I am sorry, Raymond, you're the typa
geeza should come with a warning written on
you. You're a child, Raymond. You'll cut me
again. You're a charmer, and you did reach me,
but this is not real, I don't trust it, you're running
round town fuckin this girl and that and already
I'm hurt by it and we're not even together, and I
feel rejected and ugly and I'm thinking 'bout her
if you like her better than me, and thass all I'm

fuckin thinkin 'bout since I heard, and I resent
them things, I resent them things cause I'm a
proper big woman, Raymond, you understand
me, I'm a proper big woman, I'm not fifteen,
you understand, and I'm subjugated already
by wanting you so much, and yeah, you'll say
you'll change but this is your meat and drink
picking up girls and fuckin with their heads juss
like this, I know all about this Raymond, you
get us hooked into your orbit and you shit all
over us, and I been through this, this torture
so many fuckin times I swore I'd never ask a
man to gimme pain again, and I know from one
good look at you that you can't stop, you don't
have the strength to stop hurting women and it
cuts me because there really is something about
you darling, something I've seen and I really
do think that I could love it, and I know iss the
damage that locks you into doing all this bad
stuff, I know that, but you scare me and I gotta
go, Raymond, I'm sorry, but now I really muss
duss because looking at you makes me fifteen
again and I'm getting dazzled in my belly so
this where I get off, I'm sorry because you are
so beautiful and I'm gonna walk away now,
Raymond...

RAYMOND   Don't kill me, Simone

SIMONE   I can't. I gotta go.

RAYMOND   Simone...

SIMONE   I gotta go, I can't do this, I'm sorry, Raymond, I
gotta go

RAYMOND   Simone, wait, Simone, juss give a geeza a fair
hearing, hear me out, Simone...

Song – Don't Go

I been wandering around
Foolin myself
Playin a game I didn't need to play
I been wandering around
Lying to myself
Thought I had it all

(*Spoken.*) And realised...I ain't got shit

(*Song.*) Simone I been so lonely
Shivering in this broken hearted rain
Suddenly you are there to light my path
Stripped me of my armour
And now my heart has no defence
Only you Simone can caress my soul
You're living in my heart
You know that I'm lost here
But I'm yours to find
Only you Simone can give me joy
This is my prayer
That you'll stand beside me
Or I'll go blind
Cause you're my last chance of salvation
This time I'll try harder
Harder
Cause I'm drowning in my yearning
Lift me clear and make me whole Simone

Pause.

SIMONE   Goodbye, Raymond.

SIMONE exits.

RAYMOND   Aaaahhhhhh!!!!!!!!!!!!

GIL wakes up.

82

GIL   Oi! Oi!Oi! Oi! Oi!

GIL jumps on RAYMOND in a kind of embrace.

Raymond. Raymond. Raymond. Look at me.
Look at me. It's Me, Raymond. Come on…
This isn't you, Raymond… Come Back… See?
Fever's gone…

RAYMOND has calmed down.

You gotta get out there and open your mouth
again and make a sound, don't lose this.

RAYMOND runs out the bar.

RAYMOND   Simoooooone!

Pause.

GIL   What a pair of useless fuckin twats.

Pause.

Barney?

BARNEY   (*Offstage.*) Yeah?

GIL   Where are you?

BARNEY   Cellar.

GIL   You can come out now.

BARNEY emerges from the cellar.

You hear all that?

BARNEY   Yep.

GIL   What a palaver. I thought people in love meant
to feed each other, not tear strips off each other.

BARNEY   S'juss women. S'just men.

GIL   All this time I spent building Raymond into a
notch, turns out he's a loser sameways.

BARNEY   This is a loser's bar. Two types of bar, winner's
            bars and loser's bars. Happy bars and unhappy
            bars. We was a happy bar once. Then, through
            some subtle shift in the ether, we became a
            loser's bar. Jake's, that's a winner's bar. They
            need to be among their own tribe.

GIL   You love her, doncha?

BARNEY   Love who?

GIL   That bird. Simone whatever.

BARNEY   Don't be ridiculous.

GIL   Come on… Thass my tribe. The lovelorn prats
            tribe. I can sniff out a fellow member.

BARNEY   Broken glass all over the floor.

GIL   You love her.

            YVONNE re-enters.

YVONNE   Nice night out.

GIL   The slapper's back.

YVONNE   Shutchour face, you.

BARNEY   See your mate out there?

YVONNE   Yeah. Smoking a fag, I see the two a them.
            Simone come out moving fast, he comes out
            soon after, talkin 'bout he loves, he loves her, he
            never loved nobody like he loves her, all that
            flannel. He chasin her all the road in between
            the neon and the shadows, a proper li'l drama…

BARNEY   Whass the prognosis?

YVONNE   She's into him. My girl Simone love a damaged
            man. We all do. Thass how you lot get away
            with it.

BARNEY   My ex-wife never let me get away with fuckall.
          Don't include me in that.

YVONNE   Fancy a stroll, Gil?

GIL   You're not gonna try and fuck me, are you?

YVONNE   Nah. Most probly snap you right in half. Come
          for a stroll. I'll tell you 'bout a few dreams I had.

GIL   Wherejuh wanna go?

YVONNE   Kite Hill.

GIL   I like it up there.

YVONNE   Come on then.

GIL   Can I set fire to a few rubbish bins along the
          way?

YVONNE   If you like.

GIL   Come on then.

YVONNE   Any chance of a takeaway, Barney?

BARNEY   Take as much as you can carry. We're closing
          down tonight.

YVONNE   Bless you, Barney.

          *YVONNE grabs some champagne and heads for the
          door.*

          Y'ready then, mate?

GIL   Let's do this like a boodist cos we always knew
          this.

          She touches his face

YVONNE   Gil... You're the only man I been with who I
          didn't wanna fuck.

GIL   I'm flattered. Less go.

They exit.

Song– Closing Up For Good

BARNEY   Last one to leave
Lock all the doors
Thought to myself
Love don't drink here any more
'Cause it's closing time
And I'm closing up for good

And I've tried, I've tried
When you've seen the things that I have
seen
You remember all the simple things
I've tried

One more for the road
Make it large and extra strong
My heart's about to explode
If I don't sing my own sweet song
'Cause it's closing time
And I'm closing up for good

Flip out the lights
Stack up all the chairs
Harsh winter lights
And a blast of ice cold air
Yes it's closing time
and I'm closing up for good

Neon and shadows
The lights of the street
Wailing of sirens
But life still is sweet
And it's closing time
I'm closing up for good

GIL	Ready to love again
SIMONE	Not this time no, no, no.
YVONNE	I can't wait to see what I dream tonight
RAYMOND	Only you Simone
ALL	And I've tried
	I've tried
	When you've seen the things that I have seen
	You remember all the simple things
	I've tried
	I've tried
	When you've seen the things that I have seen you just
	Stop

Fade out.

End.